SUMMARY
of
GRIT

The Power of Passion and Perseverance

by Angela Duckworth

A FastReads Book Summary with
Key Takeaways & Analysis

TABLE OF CONTENTS

BOOK OVERVIEW

INTRODUCTION

PART I: WHAT GRIT IS AND WHY IT MATTERS

    CHAPTER 1: SHOWING UP

    CHAPTER 2: DISTRACTED BY TALENT

    CHAPTER 3: EFFORT COUNTS TWICE

    CHAPTER 4: HOW GRITTY ARE YOU?

    CHAPTER 5: GRIT GROWS

PART II: GROWING GRIT FROM THE INSIDE OUT

    CHAPTER 6: INTEREST

    CHAPTER 7: PRACTICE

    CHAPTER 8: PURPOSE

    CHAPTER 9: HOPE

PART III: GROWING GRIT FROM THE OUTSIDE IN

    CHAPTER 10: PARENTING FOR GRIT

    CHAPTER 11: THE PLAYING FIELDS OF GRIT

    CHAPTER 12: A CULTURE OF GRIT

    CHAPTER 13: CONCLUSION

BOOK OVERVIEW

In the book *Grit: The Power of Passion and Perseverance*, author Angela Duckworth brings our attention to this lesser-known psychological trait called grit. Grit has two components: passion and perseverance. Passion means having enduring interest in the job you are doing. Perseverance means being persistent and never giving up. In the book, Duckworth shows how grit is important in understanding the psychology of achievement.

The Grit Scale, which measures an individual's grit score, correctly predicted which cadets at West Point would pass the Beast Barracks, which National Spelling Bee participants would advance to the next rounds, and which sales people would be able to retain their jobs.

The book also discusses how talent gets overemphasized, whereas grit gets underemphasized. When we place more emphasis on talent, we ignore everything else, including effort. In a natural vs. striver situation, we are most likely to favor the naturally gifted person, thus leading to the naturalness bias. Duckworth argues that effort counts twice. A talent with no effort is just unmet potential. She shows that how with the addition of effort, talent becomes skill, and skill when put to a productive use becomes achievement.

In order to help people cultivate a sense of passion and perseverance, the author introduces four psychological assets commonly found in the grittiest people: interest, practice, purpose, and hope. Interest and purpose are two sources of passion. Practice and hope help develop perseverance which nurtures the "never give up" attitude. This attitude, which helped cadets pass Beast at West Point, helps us follow what we have started through to the end.

Grit can be cultivated with the help of the four psychological assets or the people around us, our parents, teachers, mentors, etc. Certain parenting methods as well as extracurricular activities can also help become our children grittier.

INTRODUCTION

Author Angela Duckworth begins the book by sharing a personal life story. She reveals how in her childhood, she was constantly told by her father that she wasn't a genius. He not only underestimated her intellectual potential but also worried that she might not achieve a lot in her career.

Fast forward to 2013, when psychologist Duckworth was awarded a MacArthur Fellowship, which is also known as the "genius grant." It was after winning this award that she realized a person's accomplishments have more to do with his/her passion and perseverance than his/her talent. In her childhood, she wasn't considered smart enough to qualify for talented or gifted programs, yet she managed to accumulate degrees from some tough schools and most of all won the MacArthur Fellowship. There was something that mattered more than talent – grit. Being gritty helped her survive despite the fact that she wasn't the brightest in her classroom.

This personal experience lays the foundation for Duckworth's book, *Grit: The Power of Passion and Perseverance*.

PART I: WHAT GRIT IS AND WHY IT MATTERS

CHAPTER 1: SHOWING UP

In the first chapter, we are introduced to the United States Military Academy campus, located at West Point. To provide background, the admissions process at West Point is stringent. Just like at some top universities, a student must have outstanding academic performance as well as high SAT scores. However, there are some things that even Harvard won't require of you. For example, the applicant must begin his application in 11th grade, seek a nomination from a senator or member of Congress, and achieve top scores on the fitness assessment. Out of 14,000 applicants each year, only 1,200 men and women who meet West Point's harsh criteria are formally enrolled. It doesn't end here though. The cadets are required to go through a seven-week training program known as Beast Barracks or just Beast. This training program is so challenging both physically and emotionally that a significant number of cadets drop out at this stage, less than two months after being admitted. Overall, one in every five cadets fails to make it to graduation. However, other cadets manage to make it through the intensive training program.

So what are the traits that help a cadet make it through Beast Barracks?

In order to measure an applicant's aptitude, West Point's admission staff calculated a Whole Candidate Score based on the candidate's SAT scores, academic ranking, fitness marks, and leadership potential. This score helped West Point identify which applicant had the potential to survive their rigorous four-year program. Unfortunately, the Whole Candidate Score wasn't accurate in predicting who would survive and who wouldn't. In fact, higher Whole Candidate Scores didn't guarantee that a cadet wouldn't drop out.

What mattered more than talent was the mere act of "never giving up." The cadets who quit didn't do so because they lacked the ability to survive at West Point. In fact, it was the "never give up" attitude that helped them make it through Beast.

The Psychology of Success

In order to understand the recipe of success, Duckworth began interviewing some highly accomplished people from different fields. The question was simple: What helps you get to the top of your field? Some of the answers she received were field-specific. A businessperson, for instance, considered the ability to take financial risks and make decisions vital for success. There were, however, some common answers. Apart from talent, one trait that also mattered was a person's ability to keep trying even after failure. The highly successful people had perseverance and they never thought of *giving up*. Also, they had enduring passion for the job they were doing. Perseverance and passion are what make up grit.

The Grit Scale

At West Point, cadets were asked to take the **Grit Scale** for the first time in 2004; the test attempted to measure how gritty a cadet was. These were the findings:

• A cadet's grit score had no relationship with his or her Whole Candidate Score.

• A cadet's Whole Candidate Score didn't tell anything about his grit.

• There was no relationship between a cadet's talent and grit.

That year, a total of 71 cadets dropped out during the Beast. The grit score had proven to be a reliable predictor of who would drop out and who wouldn't. Thus, it wasn't talent or academic ranking or leadership skills or athletic ability that helped a cadet make it through the Beast; it was grit.

What about talent?

A person's talent has no relationship to his grittiness. Consider these examples:

• When contestants of the National Spelling Bee competition were asked to take the Grit Scale, it was found that kids who were grittier went furthest in the contest. Verbal intelligence was a predictor of success in the competition. But the children's verbal intelligence bore no relationship to their grit scores.

• The SAT and grit scores of a sample of Ivy League undergraduates were found to be inversely correlated.

• In the sales department of a company, the Grit Scale predicted which sales staff would stay and which would leave their jobs. Other personality traits including extroversion were not as effective as grit in predicting staff retention.

CHAPTER 2: DISTRACTED BY TALENT

What is it that makes some people successful and not others?

Francis Galton was one of the earliest psychologists who attempted to figure out the reason why some people achieve success while others don't. In a study he published in 1869, Galton concluded that the high achievers were extraordinary in three ways: their ability, zeal, and the capacity to work hard.

Galton's half cousin, Charles Darwin, held different views. He considered zeal and hard work as two far more important determinants of success than one's intellectual ability. In a letter he wrote to Galton, Darwin stated:

"For I have always maintained that, excepting fools, men did not differ much in intellect, only in zeal and hard work."

In 1907, another psychologist, William James, published an essay called *The Energies of Man* in which he insisted that:

• As human beings we only use a small part of our physical and mental resources.

• A gap exists between a person's potential and its actualization. As a result, we work below the optimum level.

• Only people who are extraordinary are able to push their resources to an extreme level of use.

What is more important, talent or effort?

Survey results show that:

• When asked what's more important to success, people were twice as likely to pick effort as an important determinant of success.

• While hiring, employers looked for hardworking employees five times as often as they looked for intelligent employees.

Contrary to the survey results mentioned above, Chia-Jung Tsay found that when it came to choosing between a natural and a striver, people favored the naturally talented person. This shows that what we say does not really correspond with what we do. People may value hardworking employees, but they have a hidden preference for the naturally gifted individuals. This is termed the naturalness bias.

The War for Talent

In a report titled *The War for Talent* published by McKinsey, talent was defined as the sum total of one's abilities, which included their intrinsic gifts, knowledge, skills, intelligence, experience, character, attitude, judgment and drive. It is not hard to notice that intrinsic gifts were mentioned first when defining talent.

The War for Talent argued that companies which promoted their most talented staff while getting rid of the least talented performed exceptionally well. It was later pointed out by journalist Duff McDonald that companies mentioned by McKinsey which followed the above strategy didn't perform very well after the publication of the report. Take Enron, for example. Enron, once called America's Most Innovative Company, had a policy of annually firing its least performing 15% employees. The company developed a narcissistic culture which proved detrimental for its long-term growth.

Is it wrong to favor the "gifted" over "strivers"?

Focusing our attention on talent only prevents us from looking at other factors that are equally important, such as grit. In fact, we somehow end up giving the message that these other factors do not matter at all.

Being talented is great, but the tests designed to measure talent – or grit – are certainly not great. As the title of the chapter suggests, talent distracts us from other things and one of them is effort.

CHAPTER 3: EFFORT COUNTS TWICE

Overemphasizing Talent

Everywhere around us, we come across people who overemphasize talent – including us! Every time someone pulls off a feat, we hastily declare him or her as being incredibly "talented." Are we right in labeling them as talented? What we are doing is overemphasizing talent and underemphasizing everything else.

The Mundanity of Excellence

Sociologist Dan Chambliss published a study titled *The Mundanity of Excellence* in which he argued that an extraordinary performance is a convergence of various small activities that, when looked in isolation, are nothing but ordinary actions. However, because these small activities are done correctly and in the same manner again and again, they combine to form a whole, a dazzling performance. In simple words, Chambliss believes that an extraordinary performance is nothing but an accumulation of mundane acts. In order to understand why we like to label people as "talented" – even when they are not – read what German philosopher Nietzsche has to say:

"No one can see in the work of the artist how it has become."

We do not want to see a person progress from being an amateur to an expert. Instead, we are interested in the complete picture. Saying that someone is "naturally gifted" saves us the trouble of comparing ourselves with them. We want to believe that they have some magical power which we do not possess, and for this very reason we cannot compete with them. In short, when we can't see how someone reached a certain level of excellence, we label them as "gifted."

What about talent?

Nietzsche likes to call them craftsmen instead of gifted or talented. Turning the pages of history, we can find innumerable examples of people who were slightly gifted. Those men acquired greatness and became what we now like to call as "geniuses."

How did they acquire greatness?

Like craftsmen, they were serious about what they were doing. Like craftsmen, they learned to build small parts properly and as nicely as possible. They gave themselves enough time for it. Those parts when combined formed a dazzling whole. Thus, greatness was acquired through effort.

The Psychology of Achievement

We have all come to believe that talent leads to success. But there's one piece missing in the equation of success. In order to figure out that missing element, let's define talent and achievement first.

• **Talent** means how quickly people are able to improve their skills when they put in the effort.

• **Achievement** takes place when people use the skills they have acquired.

As you may have already guessed, that missing piece is effort. And in case you didn't notice, effort comes twice in the equation.

Effort helps develop skill. Therefore, **Talent x Effort = Skill.**

Effort also helps put our skills to good use. Therefore, **Skill x Effort = Achievement.**

Of course, other factors, such as having a good teacher, mentor, or coach, may also matter, but this theory does not consider outside forces. It may be incomplete, but it's still helpful in understanding the psychology of success.

Examples:

John Irving was not a naturally gifted writer. The great storyteller lagged behind other students in school because of his severe dyslexia. If it took an average student an hour to read an assignment, it took Irving two to three hours. He was confident in his stamina, however, and knew he could do something repeatedly, regardless of the difficulty level. According to Irving, rewriting is what he does best now.

It was with effort that Irving became a master of his field and with effort that he became a great storyteller. The takeaway from Irving's story is that if you do something again and again, something that wasn't even natural to you can grow to be second nature. But just like Nietzsche said about his craftsmen, it doesn't happen overnight; it requires patience and perseverance.

Separating Talent and Skill

Person A is twice as talented but only half as hardworking as person B. Although both A and B might attain the same skill level, A might end up being less productive than B in the long run. This is because a striver who matches the skill level of a natural through hard work accomplishes more over time.

It is essential to separate talent and skill. Talent is natural whereas skill is acquired over time. However, without effort, both talent and skill are useless. When you put in the effort, talent becomes skill which, on adding more effort, produces achievement.

CHAPTER 4: HOW GRITTY ARE YOU?

Grit consists of two things: passion and perseverance.

Passion

Passion is often defined by people as an intense emotion or an obsession. In grit, however, we are talking about neither. When we say passion, we mean consistency over time. Passion is not like fireworks that go off in a blaze but fizzle just as quickly. Passion is like a compass that gives you direction and guides you to where you want to be. It may take you time to figure out your true passion.

The Goal Hierarchy

Many people find it difficult to answer the question, *What is your passion?* Some people find themselves pursuing several and different goals but are not exactly sure about their passion. A goal hierarchy helps understand whether your goals serve a common purpose.

The goal hierarchy has at least three levels: top-level goals, mid-level goals, and low-level goals. To understand the concept, let's look at this hierarchy of goals in reverse order.

Low-level Goals

These goals lie at the bottom of the hierarchy and are means to ends. They are specific and short-term, such as arriving at work on time or writing an email. You want to accomplish these tiny goals because they help you get something else.

Mid-level Goals

Between your top-level and low-level goals, many layers of mid-level goals may exist, depending upon your situation. A mid-level goal is the next milestone you need to achieve after meeting your low-level goals. For example, you want to arrive at work on time (low-level goal) because you want to be punctual (mid-level goal).

Top-level Goals

The goals at the top of the hierarchy are abstract, general and what we call your ultimate concern. There can only be one goal at the top of the hierarchy which serves as a compass and gives meaning to all the lower-level goals. For example, you want to arrive at work on time (low-level goal) so that you can be punctual (mid-level goal) so that you can be a better leader (top-level goal). Thus, being a better leader is your ultimate concern. A top-level goal is an ultimate end to which all the lower-level goals serve as means.

Passion is about being loyal to your ultimate concern. Grit means holding your ultimate goal for a long time.

• If you have a top-level goal but no supporting lower level goals, this is because you haven't figured out how to achieve your top-level goal. This is called positive fantasizing.

• In another case, you may have several low-level and mid-level goals that are not related to each other. This is because you haven't found a unifying top-level goal or your ultimate concern.

• In yet another case, you may have several multi-layered goal hierarchies that are not connected with each other in any way. This indicates goal conflicts.

Prioritizing Goals

In a goal hierarchy, there must be only one top-level goal. Gritty people have a coherent goal hierarchy where lower-level goals are somehow related to the top-level goal. In order to have a unified goal hierarchy, make sure your priorities are in order. Here's a modified version of Warren Buffet's exercise for prioritizing goals.

Step 1: List down your twenty-five career goals.

Step 2: Circle the five high-priority goals.

Step 3: The goals you didn't circle are what you must avoid. These act as distractions.

Step 4: Now look at your five top goals and see to what extent do they serve a common purpose? Goals that serve a common purpose form part of the same hierarchy. These goals serve as means to the same ultimate concern.

Here are a few things to keep in mind:

• You do not need to religiously follow every lower-level goal. You may remove a lower-level if it doesn't seem to be working and add a new lower-level goal instead that you think will work better and that serves the same purpose.

14

• The top-level goal, however, gets written in indelible ink. It's your compass that keeps pointing you in the right direction, and for this reason it cannot be edited or changed.

CHAPTER 5: GRIT GROWS

Does grit come from genes or experience?

Just like all other human traits, grit is influenced by genes as well as experience.

In a study involving more than two thousand pairs of twins, researchers estimated that 37% and 20% of variations in the perseverance and passion traits, respectively, were due to genetic factors. This shows that grit is partly affected by genetic factors and partly by experience.

What about talent?

Talent is also influenced by genes but not entirely. How quickly we develop a skill also depends upon experience.

Here are a few things to keep in mind regarding grit, talent, and other human traits:

• All human traits, including grit and talent, are influenced by genes as well as experience.

• There's no single gene that alone explains the variation in grit – or any human trait for that matter.

• Heritability estimates – which show the proportion of variation in a human trait caused by genetics – do tell why a person differs from the average, say average height, but they do not explain how average height has varied over time. This is because the environment in which we grow up also plays a role.

Coming back to growing grit, there are four psychological assets that the grittiest people have in common.

1. Interest: You must be passionate about something that interests you the most. The grittiest people have something that they love to do.

2. Practice: Practice requires you to do things that interest you better than you did yesterday. You must be ready to improve on your skills, regardless of how excellent you currently are. Challenging yourself to an exercise that exceeds your skill level leads to mastery.

3. Purpose: Without purpose, you may not be able to carry on your interest for a long time. Hence, it is essential to identify how your work is connected to your own well-being as well as the well-being of others.

4. Hope: Hope does not come at the last stage. In fact, it is needed at all stages and helps us see our ultimate concern through to the end. Grit loses when we are unable to get up after a setback. But when we get up, it prevails.

PART II: GROWING GRIT FROM THE INSIDE OUT

CHAPTER 6: INTEREST

'Follow your Passion'

'Follow your passion' is advice every one of us has been given at some point in time. Why must we follow our passion? Here is some scientific evidence that makes it absolutely necessary for us to do what we love. Research shows that:

• People with jobs that match their interests are more satisfied with their work and are happier in their lives.

• People with jobs matching their personal interests not only perform better at work but also help their coworkers. Such employees are more likely to stay at a job for a longer period.

• Similarly, students whose college major fit their personal interests get better grades and are more likely to stay in the course than drop out.

In reality, according to the 2014 Gallup survey, as many as two-thirds of adults in the United States admitted not being engaged at their jobs. Around the world, only 13% of adults called themselves engaged at work. This is enough evidence to conclude that very few people love what they do for a living.

To make sure your future job fits your interests and keeps you engaged at work, you must begin with fostering your passion.

The process of finding your passion is not like falling in love at first sight. In fact, finding your passion is rather a discovery phase followed by development and then deepening.

• Passion is not discovered through introspection. You have to interact with the outside world in order to see what triggers your interest. It is necessary because you never know what might capture your attention.

• The process may be long, messy, and may require a person to experiment with different things in order to figure out what interests them. One thing is true, however: you can never force yourself to like something.

• People around us who encourage us and give us positive feedback also help our interests thrive.

According to psychologist Benjamin Bloom, the skill development process has three distinct stages, with each stage lasting many years. Bloom found that all successful people go through these three phases, termed the early years, middle years, and later years.

1. Early Years: This is the phase in which we discover and develop our interests. Encouragement is important in this phase because the discoverer is still a beginner.

2. Middle Years: In this phase, we find the need to engage in laborious practice in order to bring continuous improvement in our skills. This phase teaches us self-discipline and perseverance.

3. Later Years: This is the final and the longest of the three phases. At this stage, people seek for the greater good of the society in the work they do. They find meaning and purpose in their jobs and see how they can help improve the well-being of others.

CHAPTER 7: PRACTICE

Practice is how you achieve continuous improvement in your skill. But how much practice is considered enough? How many hours of practice are we talking about? Psychologist Anders Ericsson talks about 10,000 hours of practice in a span of ten years. This is called deliberate practice. Here's how experts do it:

• They focus on specific weaknesses rather than what they already do well.

• They set challenges that exceed their skill level.

• They improve their skill by doing better than they did yesterday.

• When they seek feedback, they are interested in learning what they did wrong instead of what they did right.

In a study involving participants of the National Spelling Bee, Duckworth and Ericsson found that deliberate practice was more likely to help participants advance to further stages of the competition than other kinds of preparation. However, on average deliberate practice was rated by Bee spellers as more effortful and less enjoyable compared to other activities they engaged in for preparation. Playing Scrabble and reading books, for example, were rated effortless but enjoyable. The study did not find a relationship between 'reading for fun' – an effortless activity – and the participant's spelling skills.

In order to get the most out of deliberate practice, the following things are important:

• Knowing the basic requirements

1. A clearly defined goal

2. Concentration and effort

3. Immediate feedback

4. Repetition of work with improvement in weak areas

• Making deliberate practice a habit

• Changing the way we experience deliberate practice, by embracing the challenge rather than fearing it.

CHAPTER 8: PURPOSE

Apart from interest, purpose is another source of passion. Having purpose means having an intention to do something for the well-being of others or having an "other-centered" approach. In the grittiest people, passion depends upon both interest and purpose. Hence, their goals are not only self-oriented but also other-centered. For some people, purpose comes early in life. Others – or most of us – start out with personal interests and later add an other-centered purpose to their goals.

How much does Purpose matter?

Aristotle identified two reasons why we pursue happiness, eudaimonic and hedonic. The eudaimonic approach to happiness focuses on well-being whereas the hedonic approach to happiness focuses on pleasure-seeking. Human beings pursue both eudaimonic and hedonic happiness. Some people care more about hedonic pursuits (pleasure) whereas others care more about eudaimonic pursuits (purpose).

While exploring people's motivations behind grit, one study found that:

• Gritty people are just as likely to pursue hedonic happiness as other people.

• Hedonic happiness is moderately important for people regardless of how gritty they are.

• Gritty people are more likely to seek purpose and meaning in their lives.

Job, Career and Calling

When three bricklayers were asked what they were doing, they responded with the following answers:

• The first replied that he was laying bricks.

• The second replied that he was building a church.

• The third replied that he was building the house of God.

The different responses given by the bricklayers show that the first bricklayer saw his occupation as a job, the second saw it as a career, whereas the third saw it as a calling. People who describe their occupation as a calling are grittier than those who consider their work a career or job.

Finding Purpose

In order to find purpose and meaning in your life, you can do the following:

• Look at your present job and think how it can help other people's well-being and the society.

• Think about how you can make minor changes in your current job description to match it with your values.

• Look for a role model who can inspire you to find purpose in life.

CHAPTER 9: HOPE

Hope is an expectation that things will be better tomorrow. This hope comes without responsibility, and there's no burden on the shoulders of the person who hopes.

When we talk about grit, we are looking at a different kind of hope. This kind of hope depends on the expectation that your own efforts will change the future. Hence, the burden of responsibility lies on your shoulders. Gritty people do not bank on luck; they get up and change things.

Optimist and Pessimist

Research finds that optimists are as likely to face bad circumstances as their pessimist counterparts. They differ, however, in the way they explain their sufferings. Optimists find temporary causes to explain their suffering whereas pessimists blame their suffering on permanent causes. For example, an optimist might say, *I didn't work hard enough*, whereas a pessimist might say, *I'm a loser; I screw things up*.

We may not be aware of it, but these mindsets play an important role in how we look at life. Research findings show that:

• Optimists are less likely to suffer from anxiety and depression compared to their pessimist counterparts.

• Optimistic students earn better grades at school and are less likely to drop out.

• Optimistic young adults remain healthier in their middle-age. They are also more likely to live longer than their pessimist counterparts.

• Optimists are more likely to be satisfied with their marriages.

Fixed and Growth Mindset

Researcher Carol Dweck believes that all of us carry either a fixed or a growth mindset. People with a growth mindset believe that if they try hard enough, they can get smarter, get better grades, learn a new skill, etc. On the other hand, people with a fixed mindset don't think they have the capability to improve. In fact, in the face of difficulty, they are most likely to give up.

Carol found that people who possess a growth mindset are grittier than those who do not. A fixed mindset leads to pessimistic explanations of suffering, which can lead to giving up on the challenge entirely. A growth mindset leads to optimistic explanations of suffering, and thus leads to perseverance.

PART III: GROWING GRIT FROM THE OUTSIDE IN

CHAPTER 10: PARENTING FOR GRIT

How can you teach your children to be grittier?

We can teach our children to be grittier by fostering interest, practice, purpose, and hope in them. Although there's a lot of research available on parenting and some research available on grit, unfortunately, no researcher has studied both parenting and grit yet.

Psychologists divide parenting styles into four categories:

1. Authoritative Parenting or Wise Parenting

In the authoritative or wise parenting style, parents are both supporting and demanding. Wise parents have a fair idea of the psychological needs of their children. They are warm, respectful, and demanding.

2. Authoritarian Parenting

In the authoritarian parenting approach, parents are demanding but not supportive. Parents set high behavior expectations in order to strengthen the character of the child.

3. Neglectful Parenting

In the neglectful parenting style, parents are neither demanding not supporting. This is by far the most negative approach to parenting since parents are highly uninvolved.

4. Permissive Parenting

In the permissive parenting style, parents are undemanding but yet supportive. This approach is known as the lenient way of parenting kids.

Research has amassed a lot of evidence for the benefits of the wise parenting style. One study proves that children of wise, authoritative parents perform better in life than children raised by other kinds of parents. Children of wise parents earn better grades in school and are less likely to suffer from depression and anxiety.

Wise parents encourage their kids to emulate them. However, it is wrong to assume that all children with wise parents will grow up to be gritty. For one, not all wise parents are gritty. If you want your kids to grow up to be gritty, try to answer the following questions:

• How much perseverance and passion do you have for your own personal goals?

• Does your approach to parenting motivate your child to emulate you?

CHAPTER 11: THE PLAYING FIELDS OF GRIT

Structured extracurricular activities like ballet, piano, and football help foster grit in children. When children are playing a sport or engaged in an extracurricular activity, they are both challenged and having fun. Research indicates that kids who participate in extracurricular activities get better grades, have higher self-esteem, and are less likely to get in trouble.

Why extracurricular activities?

• Because there is an adult in charge of the activity who is not the parent.

• Because these activities are structured to foster interest, practice, purpose, and hope in kids.

CHAPTER 12: A CULTURE OF GRIT

Culture represents how and why we do certain things the way we do them. A culture can exist when a group of people decide in consensus how they should do things and why. When we adopt a certain culture, we become part of their in-group.

In order to be gritty, we can use one of two methods:

• The first way is to do it all by ourselves.

• The second way is to use conformity. In order to be grittier, we must be around people who are gritty.

Culture can influence grit through conformity in the short-term. In the long run, culture can help you shape your identity. If you want be gritty, find a culture that's gritty and join it. If you want your employees to be gritty, create a culture of grit in your workplace.

CHAPTER 13: CONCLUSION

This book attempted to bring to light what we generally ignore while relying heavily on talent – it's grit. How we achieve our long-term goals greatly depends upon our passion and perseverance toward these goals.

The book ends with the following closing thoughts:

You can grow your grit

As discussed in the book, we can grow our grit "from inside out" by using the four psychological assets: interest, practice, purpose, and hope. We can also grow our grit "from outside in" by taking the help of our parents, coaches, teachers, mentors, and our friends.

Happiness

While we strive for success, we tend to ignore happiness. The two factors may be related but they are certainly not identical. Research shows that grit is related to job satisfaction and well-being. Moreover, gritty people are more likely to lead healthy emotional lives.

Can we have too much grit?

We have been told time and again that too much or too little of something can be bad. In her research, Duckworth has not found a single person who wanted to be less gritty. Hence, the idea of possessing too much grit is exceptional and also rare.

Is grit the only thing that matters?

Sure, grit is an important aspect of character. But it is not the only thing that matters. The author identifies three important dimensions of human character: intrapersonal, interpersonal, and intellectual.

1. Intrapersonal Character

Apart from grit, it includes self-control. This dimension is predictive as far as academic achievement is concerned.

2. Interpersonal Character

This includes self-intelligence, gratitude, and self-control over emotions. This dimension becomes more important in social settings.

3. Intellectual Character

This includes curiosity, zest, and other characteristics that pertain to learning.

Here are a few things to keep in mind what it means to be *gritty*:

• Being gritty means always having one foot in front of the other.

• Being gritty means having goals that are interesting as well as purposeful.

• Being gritty means continuously challenging yourself to improve your skills.

• Finally, being gritty means falling down seven times and getting up the eighth.

END

If you enjoyed this summary, please leave 5 stars and an honest review on Amazon.com!

CPSIA information can be obtained
at www.ICGtesting.com
Printed in the USA
LVOW13s0208100517
533943LV00007BA/422/P